JOHN RUTTER

THREE SHAKESPEARE SONGS

FOR MIXED VOICES UNACCOMPANIED

OXFORD

OXFORD
UNIVERSITY PRESS

Great Clarendon Street, Oxford OX2 6DP,
United Kingdom

Oxford University Press is a department of the University of Oxford.
It furthers the University's objective of excellence in research, scholarship,
and education by publishing worldwide. Oxford is a registered trade mark of
Oxford University Press in the UK and in certain other countries

First published 2022

Impression: 1

ISBN 978–0–19–356247–9

Music originated on Sibelius
Printed in Great Britain on acid-free paper by
Halstan & Co. Ltd, Amersham, Bucks.

THREE SHAKESPEARE SONGS

JOHN RUTTER

1. O mistress mine

Twelfth Night, Act II scene 3

* Dotted rhythms should be relaxed, like triplets.

Printed in Great Britain

OXFORD UNIVERSITY PRESS MUSIC DEPARTMENT, GREAT CLARENDON STREET, OXFORD OX2 6DP

4

*The melody line, in the tenor part, is omitted from here until bar 26 and between bars 42 and 44, in the interests of playability.

6

2. Be not afeard

The Tempest, Act III scene 2

*These three voice parts should be balanced equally. The 2nd soprano part may be taken by 1st altos, or other reassignments of individual voices applied.

14

3. Sigh no more, ladies

Much Ado about Nothing, Act II scene 3

*The melody line, in the tenor part, is omitted from here until bar 70 in the interests of playability.

23 April 2021
Shakespeare's birthday